© CONTENTS

In this activity book you'll find 100 key words for you to learn to read in Urdu. All of the activities are designed specifically for reading non-Latin script languages. Many of the activities are inspired by the kind of games used to teach children to read their own language: flashcards, matching games, memory games, joining exercises, etc. This is not only a more effective method of learning to read a new script, but also much more fun.

We've included a **Scriptbreaker** to get you started. This is a friendly introduction to the Urdu script that will give you tips on how to remember the letters.

Then you can move on to the 8 **Topics**. Each topic presents essential words in large type. There is also a pronunciation guide so you know how to say the words. These words are also featured in the tear-out **Flashcard** section at the back of the book. When you've mastered the words, you can go on to try out the activities and games for that topic.

There's also a **Round-up** section to review all your new words and the **Answers** to all the activities to check yourself.

Follow this 4-step plan for maximum success:

1 Have a look at the key topic words with their pictures. Then tear out the flashcards and shuffle them. Put them Urdu side up. Try to remember what the word means and turn the card over to check with the English. When you can do this, cover the pronunciation and try to say the word and remember the meaning by looking at the Urdu script only.

2 Put the cards English side up and try to say the Urdu word. Try the cards again each day both ways around. (When you can remember a card for 7 days in a row, you can file it!)

3 Try out the activities and games for each topic. This will reinforce your recognition of the key words.

4 After you have covered all the topics, you can try the activities in the Round-up section to test your knowledge of all the Urdu words in the book. You can also try shuffling all the flashcards together to see how many you can remember.

This flexible and fun way of reading your first words in Urdu should give you a head start whether you're learning at home or in a group.

The 100 Word

Book

u

... e Wightwick

... hammed Ashraf and

... ngat Bhardwaj

g-and-W
PUBLISHING

Published by *g-and-w* PUBLISHING
47a High Street
Chinnor
Oxfordshire OX9 4DJ

First published 2000

© *g-and-w* PUBLISHING 2000

ISBN 1-903103-06-1

Designed by: Robert Bowers

Illustrated by: Mahmoud Gaafar

Printed in Hong Kong
by Wing King Tong Co. Ltd.

2 3 4 5 6 7 8 9 09 08 07 06 05 04 03 02

SCRIPTBREAKER

The purpose of this Scriptbreaker is to introduce you to the Urdu script and how it is formed. You should not try to memorise the alphabet at this stage, nor try to write the letters yourself. Instead, have a quick look through this section and then move on to the topics, glancing back if you want to work out the letters in a particular word. Remember, though, that recognising the whole shape of a word in an unfamiliar script is just as important as knowing how it is made up. Using this method you will have a much instinctive recall of vocabulary and will gain the confidence to expand your knowledge in other directions.

The Urdu script is not nearly as difficult as it might seem at first glance. There are 37 letters in total, no capital letters, and, unlike English, words are spelled as they sound. There are two main points to commit to your brain:

- Urdu is written from right to left.

- The letters are "joined up" — you cannot "print" a word as you can in English.

The alphabet

The easiest way of tackling the alphabet is to divide it into similarly shaped letters. For example, here are two groups of similar letters. The only difference between them is the dots:

ح (the letter *hay*)   ب (the letter *bay*)

ج (the letter *jeem*)   پ (the letter *pay*)

چ (the letter *chay*)   ت (the letter *tay*)

خ (the letter *khay*)   ث (the letter *say*)

When these letters join to others letters they change their shape. The most common change is that they lose their "tails":

$$ خچ = ج + ت \qquad جب = ب + ج \qquad \text{(read from right to left)} \longleftarrow $$

Because letters change their shape like this, they have an initial, a medial (middle) and a final form. For example, the letter ج (*jeem*) changes like this;

- at the beginning of a word (initial) ج

- in the middle of a word (medial) ج

- at the end of a word (final) ج

5

- ✔ Urdu has 37 letters and no capital letters
- ✔ Urdu reads right to left
- ✔ Urdu is written in "joined up" writing
- ✔ The "tail" is generally chopped off before joining the next letter.

A few letters change shapes completely depending on where they fall in a word. For example, the letter غ (ghain) changes like this:

| initial غـ | medial ـغـ | final ـغ |

In addition, there are 10 letters which never join to the letter following (to their left) and so hardly change shape at all.

و (vao)   ر (ray)   ڑ (Ray)   ز (zay)   ژ (Zay)

ا (alif)   د (dal)   ڈ (Dal)   ذ (zal)   ے (baRii yai)

You will find more details of how the individual letters change their shapes in the table on page 8.

◎ Formation of words

We can use the principles of joining letters to form words. So, for example, the Urdu for farm is written like this

⟵ (f) ف + (aa) ا + (r) ر + (m) م = فارم (faarm)

And the Urdu word for "shop" is written like this:

⟵ (d) د + (k) ک + (aa) ا + (n) ن = دُكان (dukaan)

You may have noticed that one of the vowels in the word *dukaan* is written above the main script. In Urdu the three short vowels (*a, i, u*) are not written as part of the script but as vowel signs above or below the letters. The short *a* is written as a stroke above the letter (َ); the short *i* as a stroke below (ِ); and the short *u* as a comma-shape above (ُ). This is similar to English speedwriting, where we might write "bnk" instead of "bank".

In this book we have included these vowel signs where necessary and the pronunciation guides will also help you. Most material for native speakers will leave them out and this makes it all the more important for you to start recognising a word without the short vowels.

- ✔ Urdu letters have an initial, medial (middle) and final form, depending on their position in the word
- ✔ Many Urdu letters simply lose their tails for the medial and final form
- ✔ A few letters change their shape completely
- ✔ 10 letters don't join to the letter after and hardly change at all
- ✔ The short vowels (*a, i, u*) are written as signs above and below the letter and are not usually included in modern written Urdu

Pronunciation tips

This activity book has simplified some aspects of pronunciation in order to emphasize the basics. Don't worry at this stage about being precisely correct — the other letters in a word will help you to be understood. Many Urdu letters are pronounced in a similar way to their English equivalents, but here are a few that need specific attention:

ص (saud) a strong "s" pronounced with the tongue on the roof of the mouth rather than up against the teeth

ض (zuad) a strong "z" pronounced with the tongue on the roof of the mouth

ط (toay) a strong "t" pronounced with the tongue on the roof of the mouth

ظ (zoay) a strong "z" pronounced with the tongue on the roof of the mouth

ڑ (Ray) a strong "r" pronounced with the tongue on the roof of the mouth

ڈ (Daal) a strong "d" pronounced with the tongue on the roof of the mouth

ح (hay) pronounced as a breathy "h"

خ (khay) pronounced as in "khaki"

ع (ain) this is a sort of guttural "ah" sound

غ (ghain) pronounced in the throat like the French "r" as in "rue"

ء (hamza) strange "half letter", not really pronounced at all, but has the effect of cutting short the previous letter

آ (maad) a long *aa* sound

7

Another important aspect of Urdu pronunciation is aspirated letters. These letters are spoken with a strong breathy sound. In the Urdu srcript they are shown by putting ھ after the letter, which is written as an elevated ^{h} in the pronunciation guide:

بھاری (b^haarii) heavy   کھڑکی (k^hiRkee) window

Summary of the Urdu alphabet

The table below shows all the Urdu letters in the three positions, with the Urdu letter name, followed by the sound. Remember that this just for reference and you shouldn't expect to take it all in at once. If you know the basic principles of how the Urdu script works, you will slowly come to recognise the individual letters.

	Ind.	final	medial	initial		Ind.	final	medial	initial		Ind.	final	medial	initial
alif *a/u/i/aa*	ا	ـا			ray *r*	ر	ـر			ghain *gh*	غ	ـغ	ـغـ	غـ
bay *b*	ب	ـب	ـبـ	بـ	Ray *R*	ڑ	ـڑ			fay *f*	ف	ـف	ـفـ	فـ
pay *p*	پ	ـپ	ـپـ	پـ	zay *z*	ز	ـز			qaaf *q*	ق	ـق	ـقـ	قـ
tay *t*	ت	ـت	ـتـ	تـ	Zay *Z*	ژ	ـژ			kaaf *k*	ک	ـک	ـکـ	کـ
Tay *T*	ٹ	ـٹ	ـٹـ	ٹـ	seen *s*	س	ـس	ـسـ	سـ	gaaf *g*	گ	ـگ	ـگـ	گـ
Say *s*	ث	ـث	ـثـ	ثـ			ـس	ـسـ	سـ	laam *l*	ل	ـل	ـلـ	لـ
jeem *j*	ج	ـج	ـجـ	جـ	sheen *sh*	ش	ـش	ـشـ	شـ	meem *m*	م	ـم	ـمـ	مـ
chay *ch*	چ	ـچ	ـچـ	چـ			ـش	ـشـ	شـ	noon *n*	ن	ـن	ـنـ	نـ
Hay *h*	ح	ـح	ـحـ	حـ	suaad *s*	ص	ـص	ـصـ	صـ	wao *w/o/oo*	و	ـو		
Khay *Kh*	خ	ـخ	ـخـ	خـ	zuaad *z*	ض	ـض	ـضـ	ضـ	hay *h*	ہ	ـہ	ـہـ	ہـ
daal *d*	د	ـد			toay *t*	ط	ـط	ـطـ	طـ	hamzaa	ء			
Daal *D*	ڈ	ـڈ			zoay *z*	ظ	ـظ	ـظـ	ظـ	yay *y/ii*	ی	ـی	ـیـ	یـ
Zaal *z*	ذ	ـذ			ain *'*	ع	ـع	ـعـ	عـ	baRii yay *e/ai*	ے	ـے	ـیـ	یـ

① AROUND THE HOME

Look at the pictures of things you might find in a house.
Tear out the flashcards for this topic.
Follow steps 1 and 2 of the plan in the introduction.

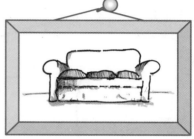

کھڑکی k^hiRkee

کُرسی kursee

میز mez

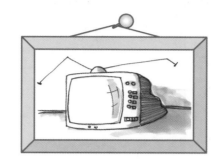

ٹیلی ویژن
Taileevizan

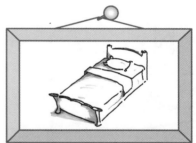

صوفہ sofaa

کمپیوٹر
kampyooTar

ٹیلی فون
Taileefon

بستر bistar

فرِج
freej

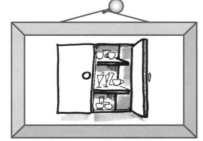

الماری
almaaree

دروازہ
darvaazaa

چُولھا chuulhaa

9

Match the pictures with the words, as in the example.

صوفہ
بستر
کھڑکی
میز
ٹیلی ویژن
کمپیوٹر
ٹیلی فون
کُرسی

Now match the Urdu household words to the English.

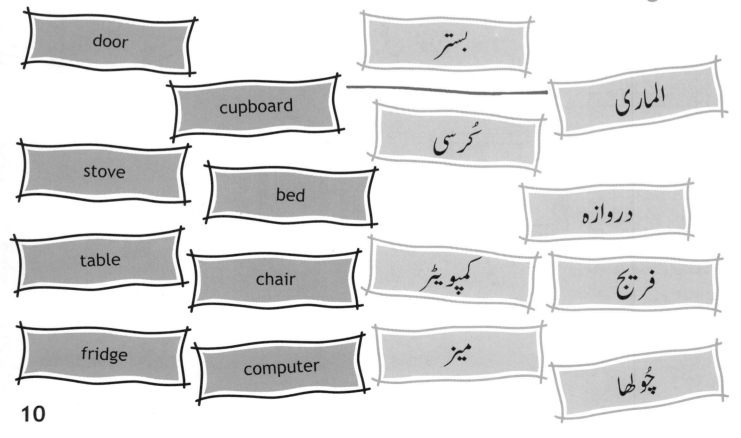

door

cupboard

بستر

الماری

stove

bed

کُرسی

دروازہ

table

chair

کمپیوٹر

فرتج

fridge

computer

میز

چُولھا

Match the words and their pronunciation.

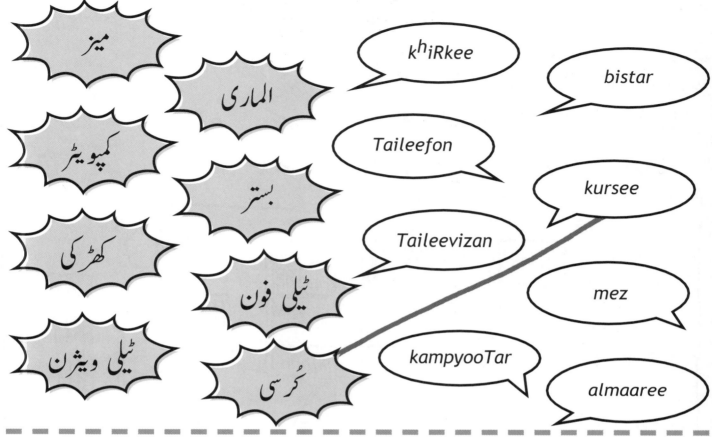

See if you can find six household words in the jumble.

ٹی شرٹ   ہوٹل

قمیض   چُولھا   گھوڑا

بستر   کھیت

ٹیکسی   ریل گاڑی   دروازہ   بائیسِکل   فرِج

خرگوش   درخت   گندا   پہاڑی

جنگل   مہنگا   صوفہ   ہلکا   آہستہ   کُرسی   بھاری

چھوٹا

11

Decide where the household items should go. Then write the correct number in the picture, as in the example.

4	ٹیلی ویژن	3	صوفہ	2	کُرسی	1	میز
8	چُولھا	7	الماری	6	بستر	5	ٹیلی فون
12	دروازہ	11	کھڑکی	10	کمپیوٹر	9	فرتیج

Now see if you can fill in the household word at the bottom of the page by choosing the correct Urdu.

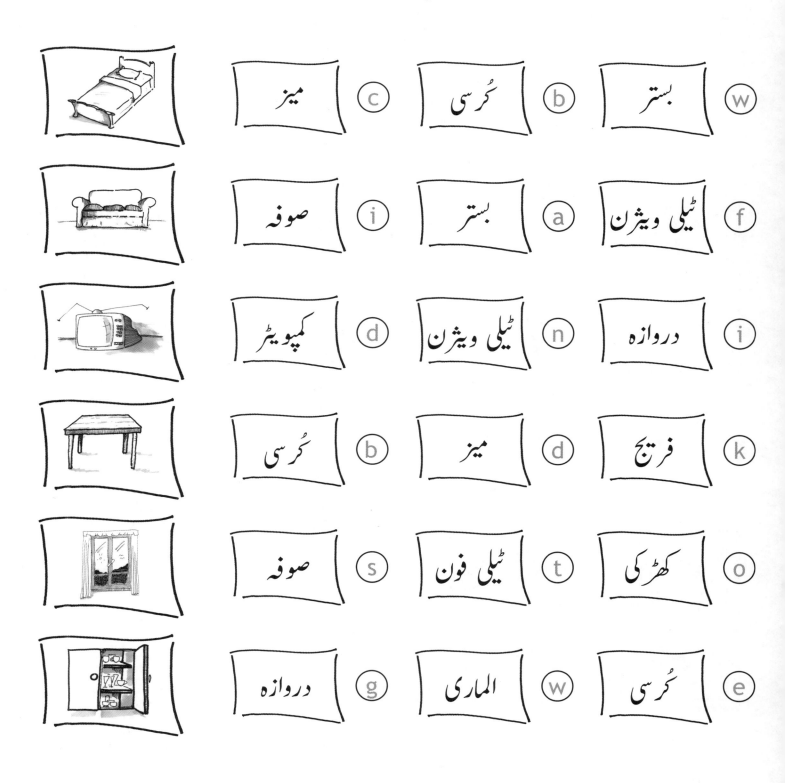

c ميز	b كُرسی	w بستر
i صوفہ	a بستر	f ٹیلی ویژن
d کمپیوٹر	n ٹیلی ویژن	i دروازہ
b كُرسی	d ميز	k فرتج
s صوفہ	t ٹیلی فون	o كھڑكی
g دروازہ	w الماری	e كُرسی

English word: Ⓦ ◯ ◯ ◯ ◯ ◯

2 CLOTHES

Look at the pictures of different clothes.
Tear out the flashcards for this topic.
Follow steps 1 and 2 of the plan in the introduction.

پیٹی peTee

سویٹر swaiTar

جُراب juraab

ٹی شرٹ Tee sharT

جانگھیا jaañghiyaa

پتلون patloon

لِباس libaas

ہیٹ haiT

کوٹ koT

سکرٹ skarT

جُوتا jootaa

قمیض kameez

Match the Urdu words and their pronunciation.

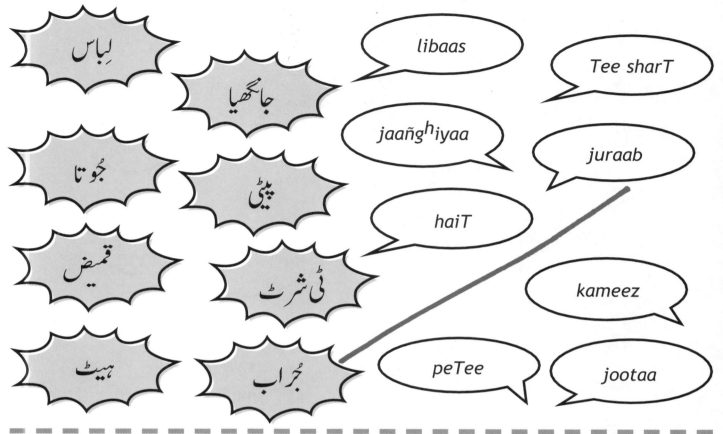

لِباس

جانگھیا

جُوتا

پیٹی

قمیض

ٹی شرٹ

ہیٹ

جُراب

libaas

Tee sharT

jaañghiyaa

juraab

haiT

kameez

peTee

jootaa

See if you can find these clothes in the word jumble.

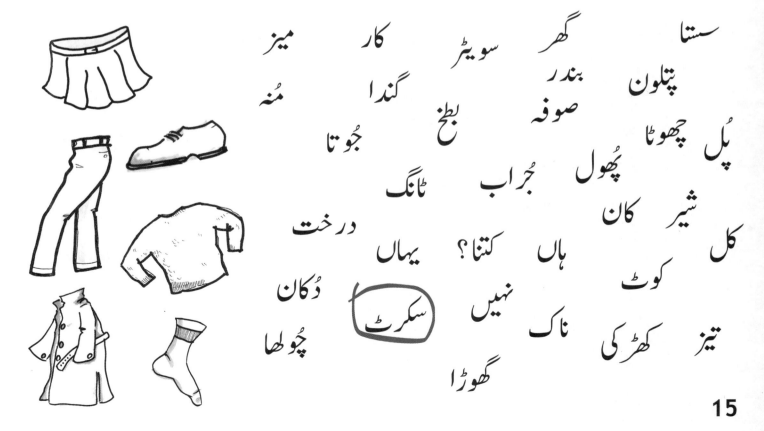

ستا	گھر	سویٹر	کار میز
پتلون	بندر		گندا مُنہ
پُل چھوٹا		صوفہ	بطخ جُوتا
شیر کان	پُھول	جُراب	ٹانگ
کل	ہاں	کتنا؟	یہاں
کوٹ		نہیں	سکرٹ
تیز کھڑکی	ناک		

درخت

دُکان

چُولھا

گھوڑا

Now match the Urdu words, their pronunciation, and the English meaning, as in the example.

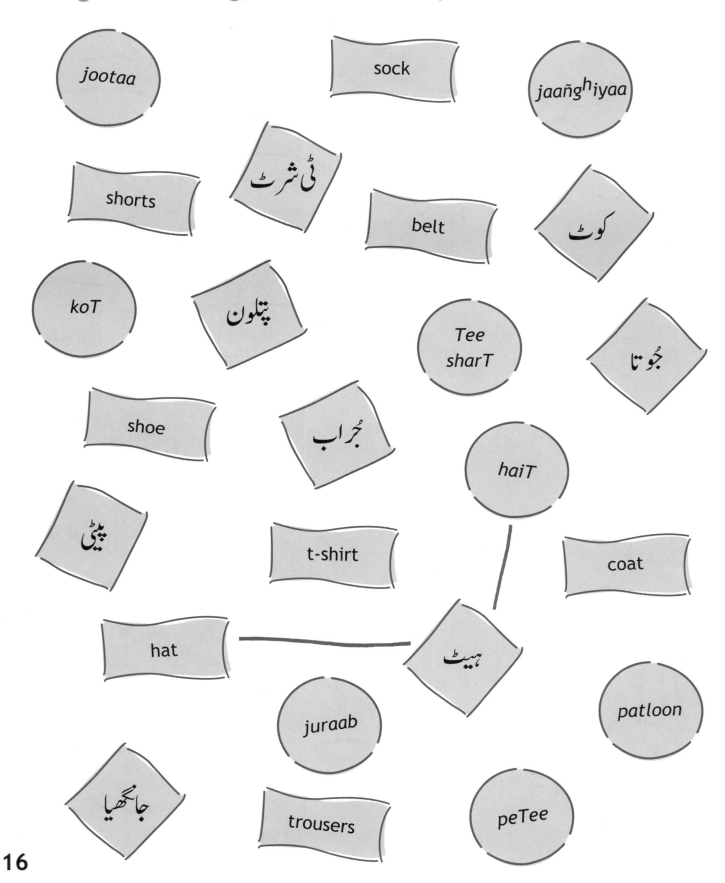

jootaa

sock

jaañgʰiyaa

ٹی شرٹ

shorts

belt

کوٹ

koT

پتلون

Tee sharT

جُوتا

shoe

جُراب

haiT

پیٹی

t-shirt

coat

hat

ہیٹ

patloon

juraab

جانگھیا

trousers

peTee

Candy is going on holiday. Count how many of each type of clothing she is packing in her suitcase.

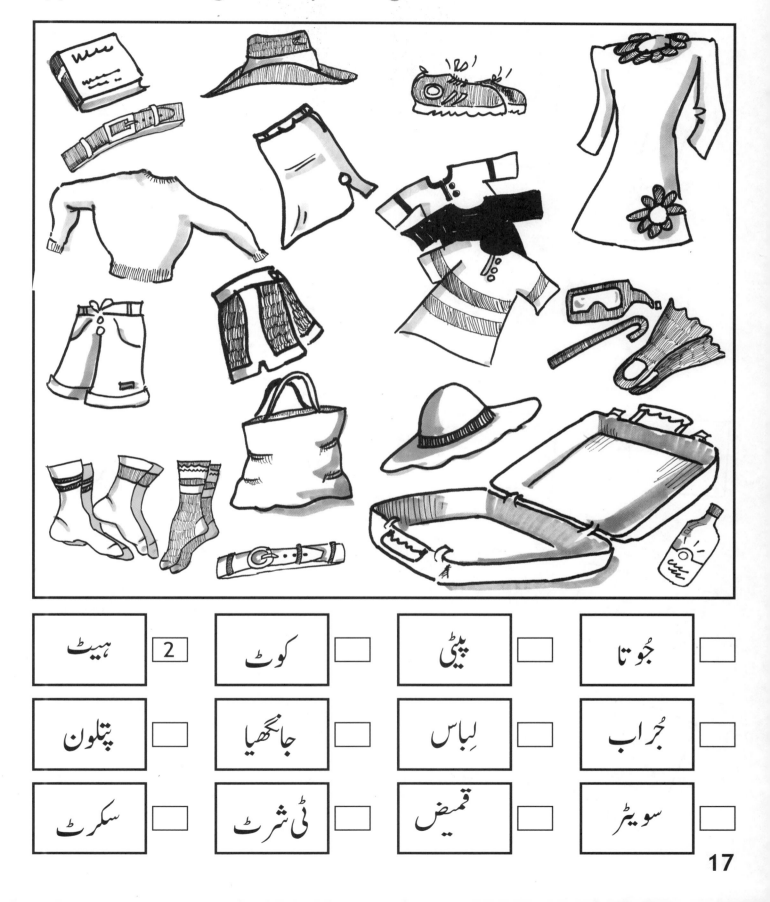

	هیٹ	2		کوٹ			پیٹی			جُوتا	
	پتلون			جانگھیا			لِباس			جُراب	
	سکرٹ			ٹی شرٹ			قمیض			سویٹر	

Someone has ripped up the Urdu words for clothes.
Can you join the two halves of the words, as the example?

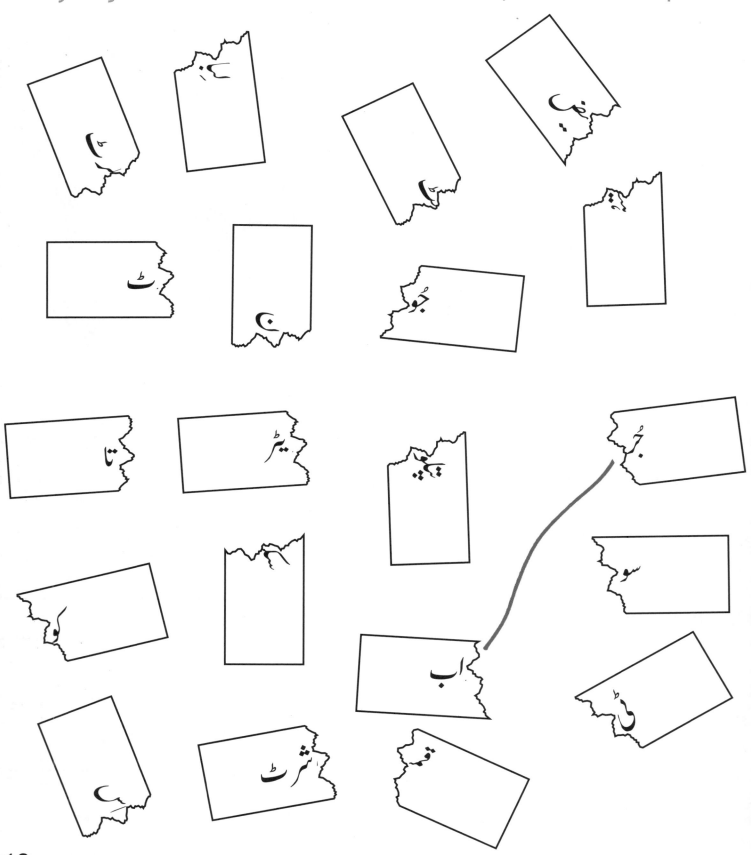

❸ AROUND TOWN

Look at the pictures of things you might see around town.
Tear out the flashcards for this topic.
Follow steps 1 and 2 of the plan in the introduction.

ہوٹل   hoTal

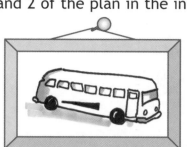

لاری   laarii

گھر g^har

کار   kaar

سینما   saneemaa

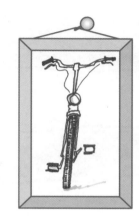

بائیسِکِل   baaisikal

ریل گاڑی
rel gaaRii

ٹیکسی   Taiksii

سکُول   skool

سڑک   saRak

دُکان   dukaan

ریسٹورینٹ
raisTorainT

Match the Urdu words to their English equivalents.

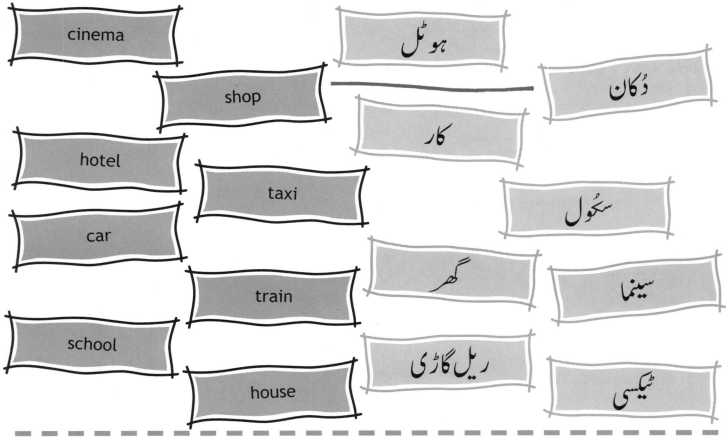

cinema

shop

ہوٹل

دُکان

کار

hotel

taxi

سکُول

car

سینما

train

گھر

school

ریل گاڑی

house

ٹیکسی

Now put the English words in the same order as the Urdu word chain, as in the example.

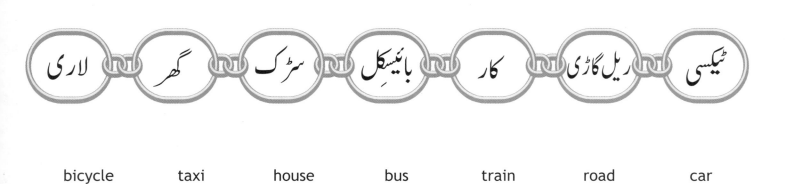

ٹیکسی	ریل گاڑی	کار	بائیسِکل	سڑک	گھر	لاری

bicycle   taxi   house   bus   train   road   car

4 ____   ____   ____   ____   ____   ____

Match the words to the signs.

لاری   بائیسِکِل   کار   سکُول

ٹیکسی   ہوٹل   ریل گاڑی   ریسٹورینٹ

Now choose the Urdu word that matches the picture to fill in the English word at the bottom of the page.

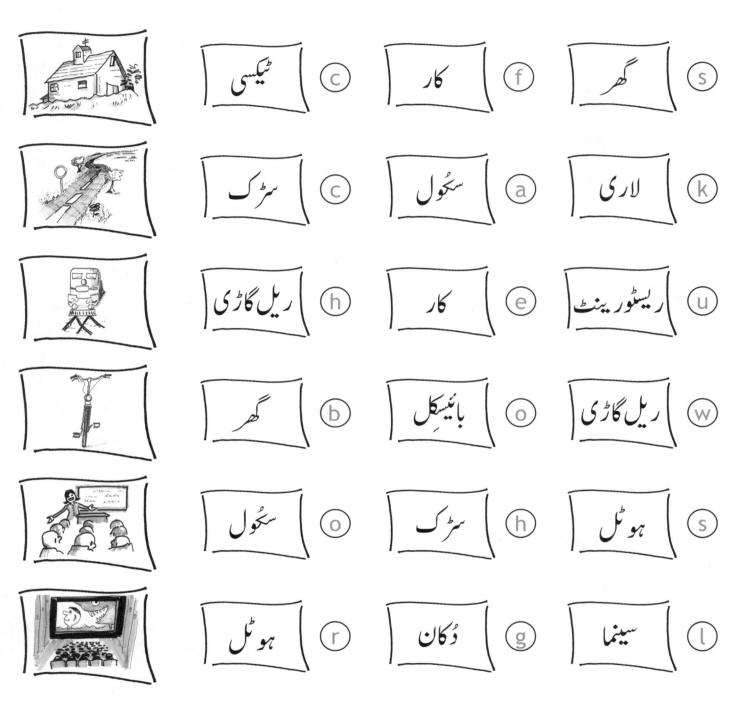

ٹیکسی	c	کار	f	گھر	s
سڑک	c	سکُول	a	لاری	k
ریل گاڑی	h	کار	e	ریسٹورینٹ	u
گھر	b	بائیسِکل	o	ریل گاڑی	w
سکُول	o	سڑک	h	ہوٹل	s
ہوٹل	r	دُکان	g	سینما	l

English word:    s ◯ ◯ ◯ ◯ ◯

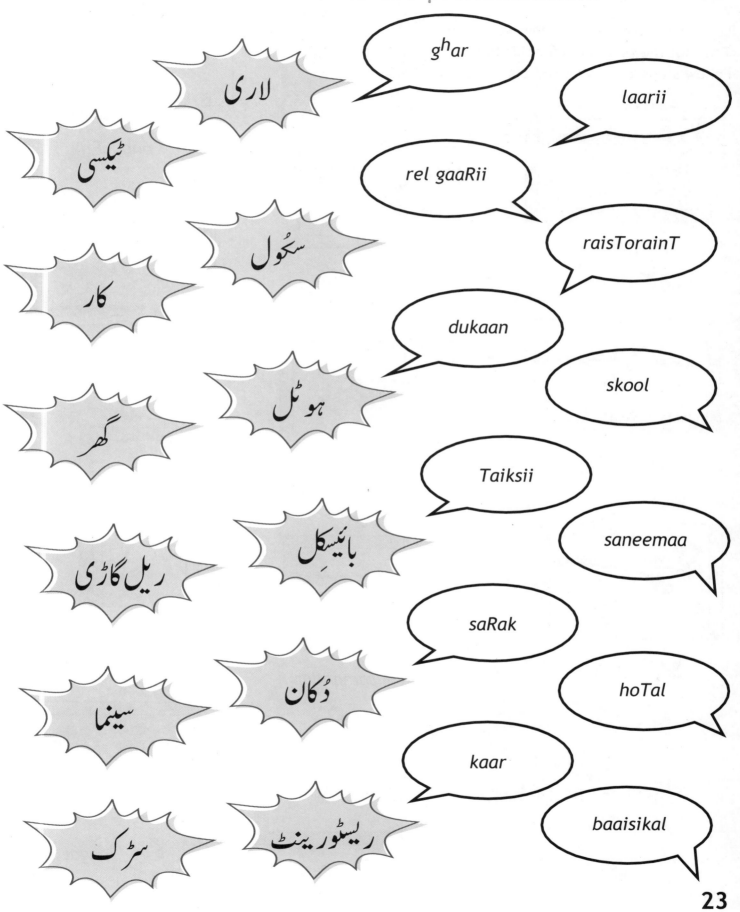

④ COUNTRYSIDE

Look at the pictures of things you might find in the countryside.
Tear out the flashcards for this topic.
Follow steps 1 and 2 of the plan in the introduction.

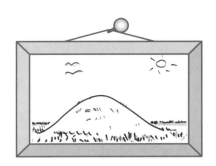

پہاڑی *pahaaRii*

پُل *pul*

فارم *faarm*

پہاڑ *pahaaR*

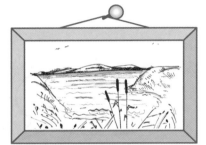

جھیل *jʰeel*

درخت *darakht*

پُھول *pʰool*

دریا *daryaa*

سمندر *samandar*

کھیت *kʰet*

صحرا *sahraa*

جنگل *jangal*

24

Can you match all the countryside words to the pictures.

پہاڑ

فارم

سمندر

جنگل

صحرا

پہاڑی

جھیل

پُل

دریا

پُھول

درخت

کھیت

Now tick (✔) the features you can find in this landscape.

پہاڑی ☐	صحرا ☐	درخت ☐	پُل ✔
جنگل ☐	کھیت ☐	سمندر ☐	پہاڑ ☐
فارم ☐	پُھول ☐	دریا ☐	جھیل ☐

Match the Urdu words and their pronunciation.

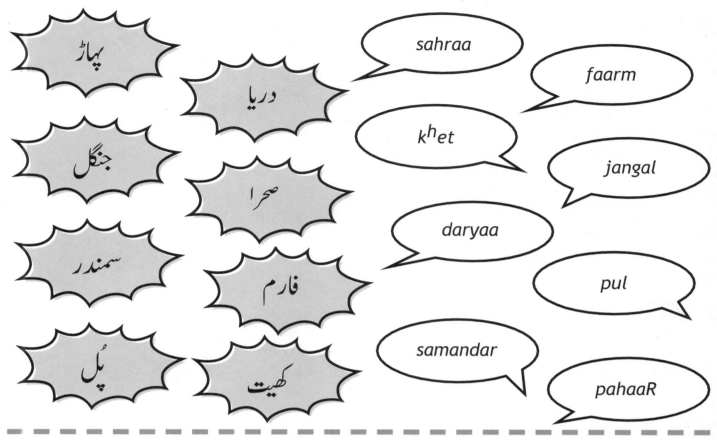

پہاڑ

دریا

sahraa

faarm

جنگل

k^het

صحرا

jangal

سمندر

فارم

daryaa

pul

پُل

کھیت

samandar

pahaaR

See if you can find these pictures in the word puzzle.

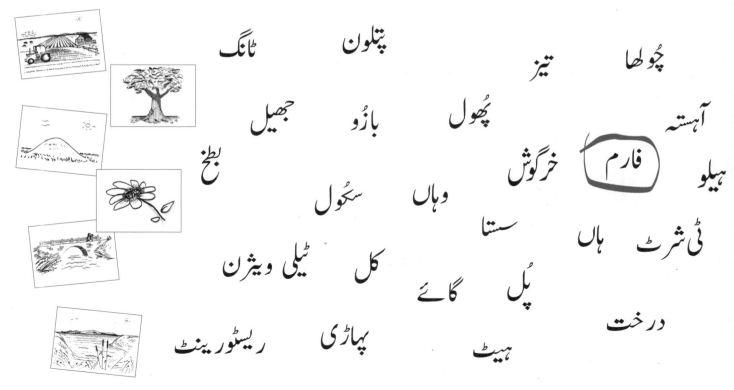

چُولھا   تیز   پتلون   ٹانگ

آہستہ   جھیل   بازُو   پھُول

ہیلو   فارم   خرگوش   بطخ

ٹی شرٹ   ہاں   سستا   وہاں   سکُول

پُل   گائے   کل   ٹیلی ویژن

درخت

ہیٹ   پہاڑی   ریسٹورینٹ

© **F**inally, test yourself by joining the Urdu words, their pronunciation, and the English meanings, as in the example.

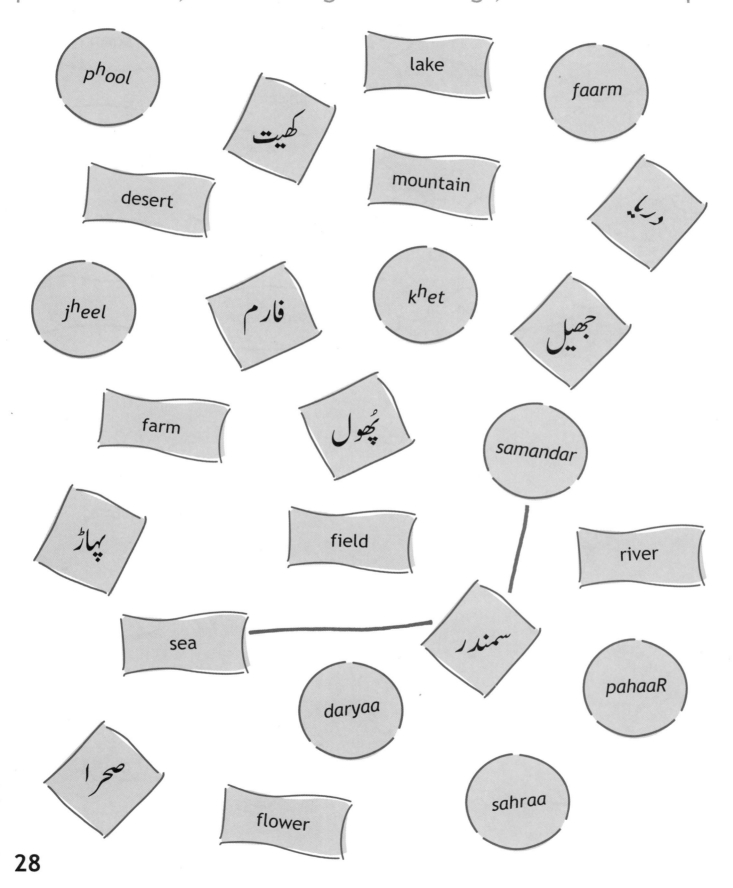

28

⑤ OPPOSITES

Look at the pictures.
Tear out the flashcards for this topic.
Follow steps 1 and 2 of the plan in the introduction.

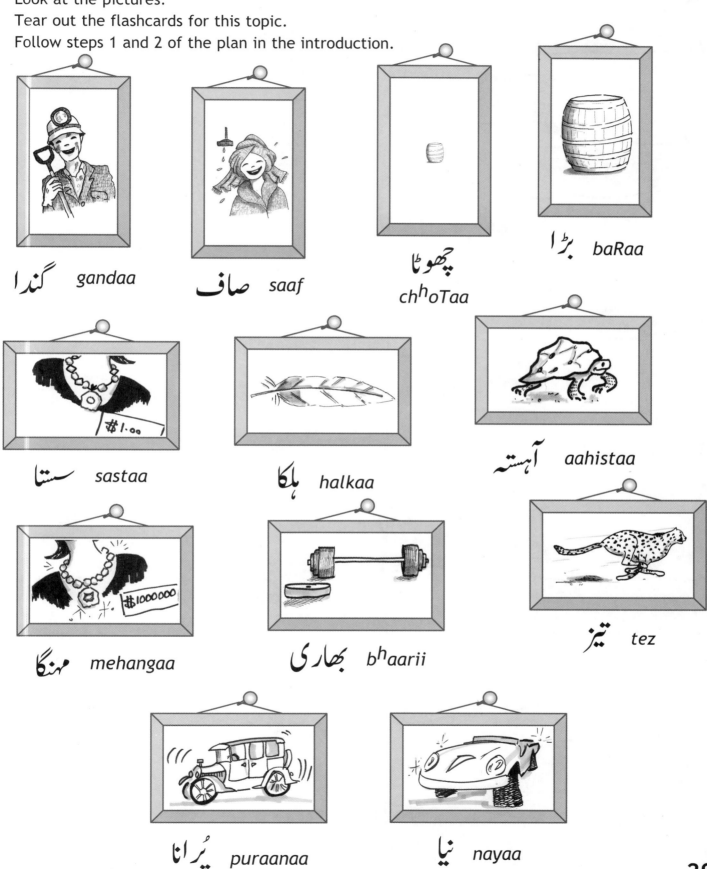

گندا gandaa

صاف saaf

چھوٹا ch^{h}oTaa

بڑا baRaa

ستا sastaa

ہلکا halkaa

آہستہ aahistaa

مہنگا mehangaa

بھاری b^{h}aarii

تیز tez

پُرانا puraanaa

نیا nayaa

Join the Urdu words to their English equivalents.

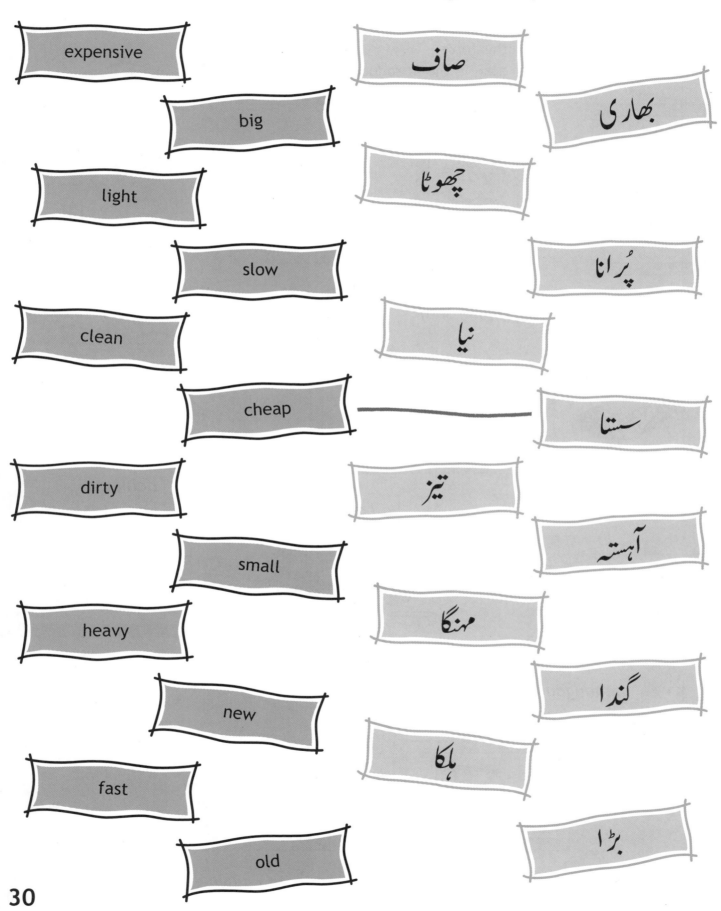

expensive

big

صاف

بھاری

light

چھوٹا

slow

پُرانا

clean

نیا

cheap ———————— سستا

dirty

تیز

آہستہ

small

heavy

مہنگا

گندا

new

fast

ہلکا

old

بڑا

Now choose the Urdu word that matches the picture to fill in the English word at the bottom of the page.

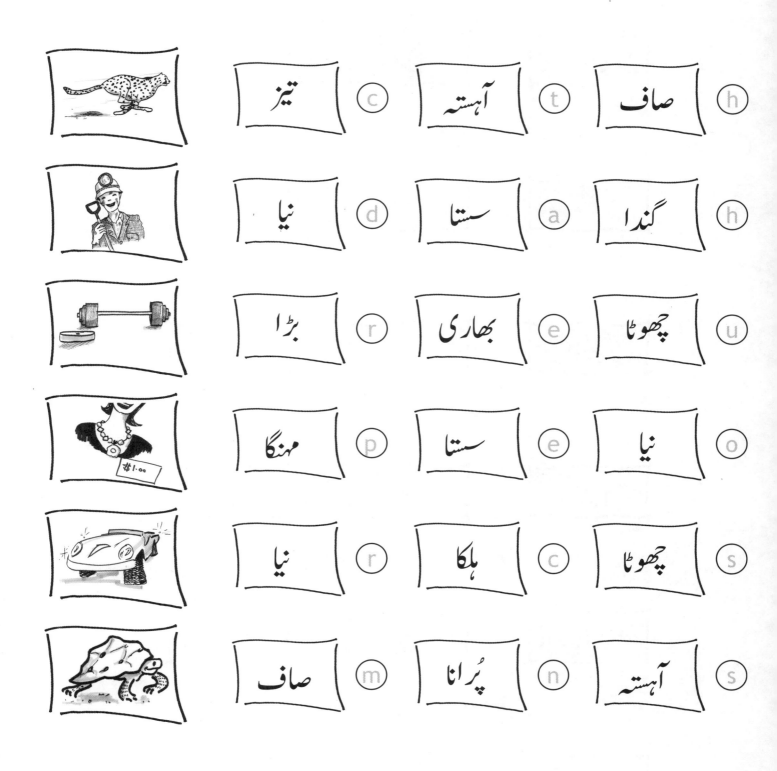

English word: ◯ ◯ ◯ ◯ ◯ !

Find the odd one out in these groups of words.

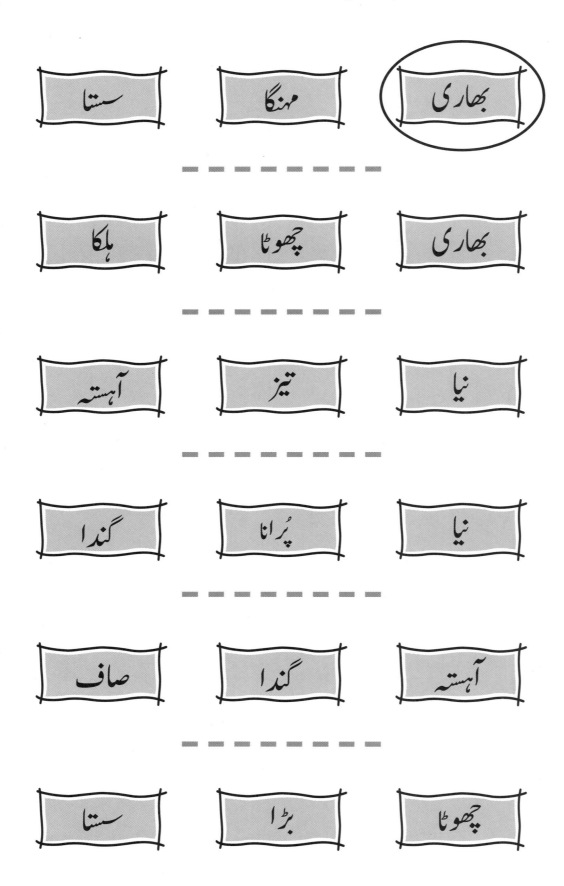

Finally, join the English words to their Urdu opposites, as in the example.

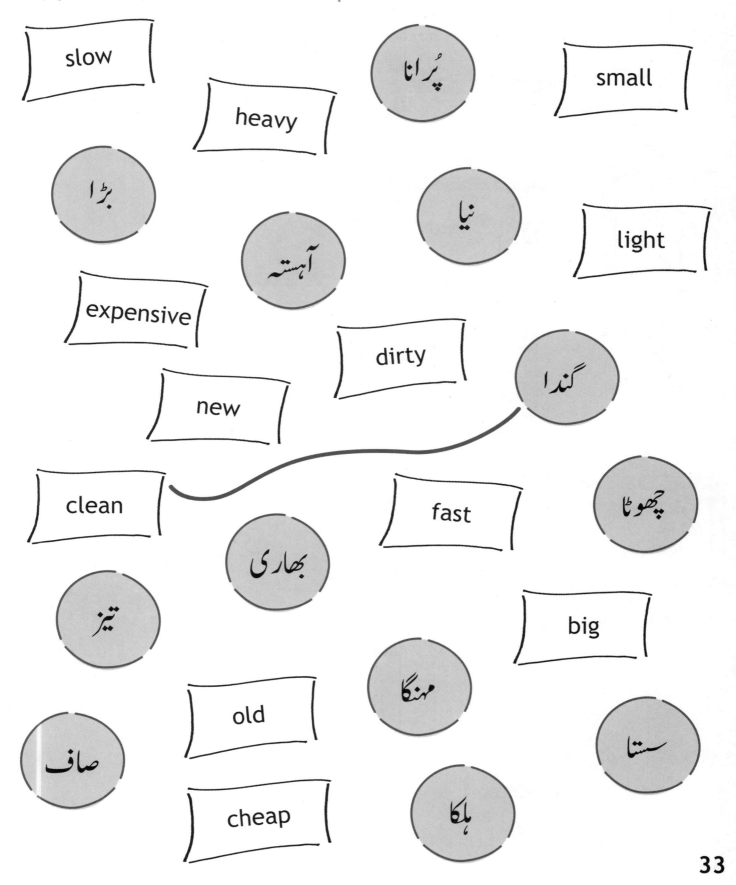

slow

پُرانا

small

heavy

بڑا

نیا

light

آہستہ

expensive

dirty

گندا

new

clean

fast

چھوٹا

بھاری

تیز

big

old

مہنگا

ستا

صاف

cheap

ہلکا

❻ ANIMALS

Look at the pictures.
Tear out the flashcards for this topic.
Follow steps 1 and 2 of the plan in the introduction.

بطخ *batakh*

ہاتھی *haathii*

بلّی *billii*

کتّا *kuttaa*

خرگوش

khargosh

بندر *bandar*

مچھلی *mach^halii*

بھیڑ *b^heR*

چُوہا *chuuhaa*

گائے *gaaye*

گھوڑا *g^hoRaa*

شیر *sher*

34

Match the animals to their associated pictures, as in the example.

خرگوش

گھوڑا

بندر

بِلّی

بھیڑ

چُوہا

کُتّا

شیر

مچھلی

گائے

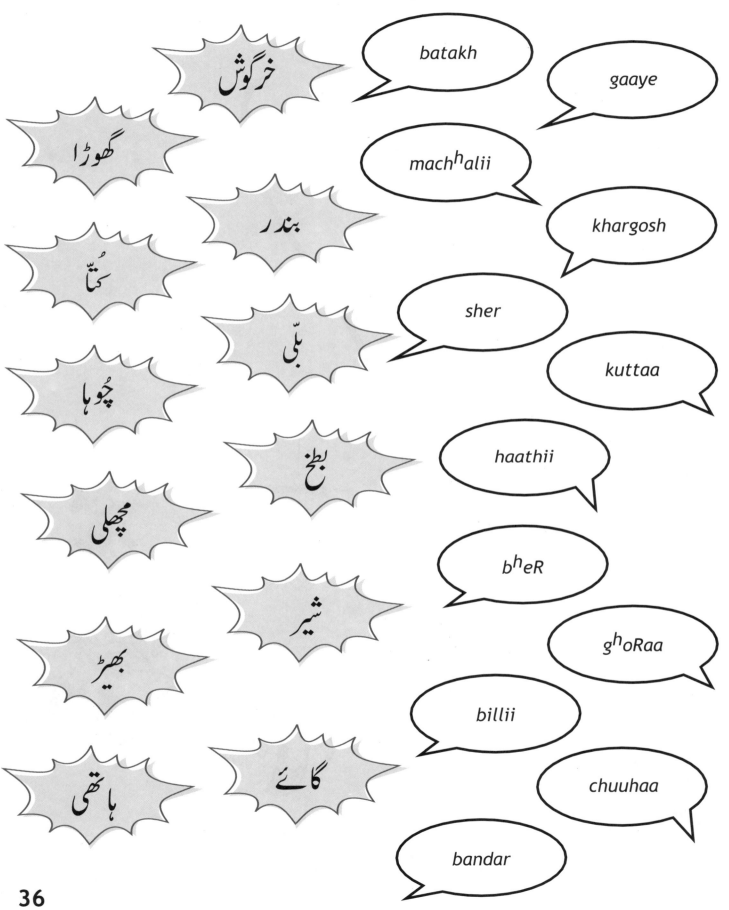

Tick (✔) the animal words you can find in the word pile.

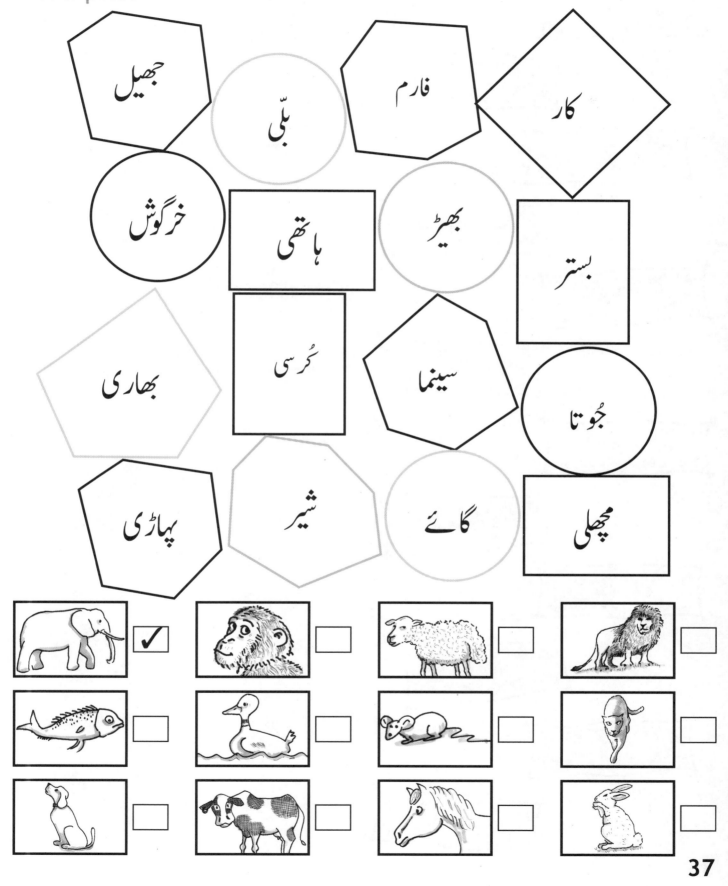

جھیل

بِلّی

فارم

کار

خرگوش

ہاتھی

بھیڑ

بستر

بھاری

کُرسی

سینما

جُوتا

پہاڑی

شیر

گائے

مچھلی

Join the Urdu animals to their English equivalents.

monkey

cow

mouse

dog

sheep

fish

lion

elephant

cat

duck

rabbit

horse

کُتّا

شیر

بندر

ہاتھی

خرگوش

مچھلی

چُوہا

بطخ

گائے

بھیڑ

گھوڑا

بلّی

❼ PARTS OF THE BODY

Look at the pictures of parts of the body.
Tear out the flashcards for this topic.
Follow steps 1 and 2 of the plan in the introduction.

 اُنگلی *ungalee*

 سر *sar*

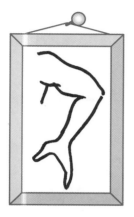 بازُو *baazuu*

 آنکھ *aañk^h*

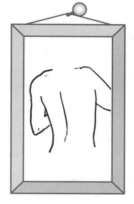 پیٹھ *peeT^h*

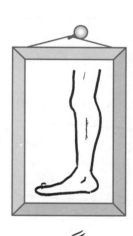 ٹانگ *Taañg*

 ہاتھ *haat^h*

 بال *baal*

 پیٹ *peT*

 کان *kaan*

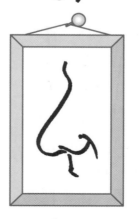 ناک *naak*

 مُنہ *mooñh*

Someone has ripped up the Urdu words for parts of the body. Can you join the two halves of the word again?

🌀 **S**ee if you can find and circle six parts of the body in the word puzzle, then draw them in the boxes below.

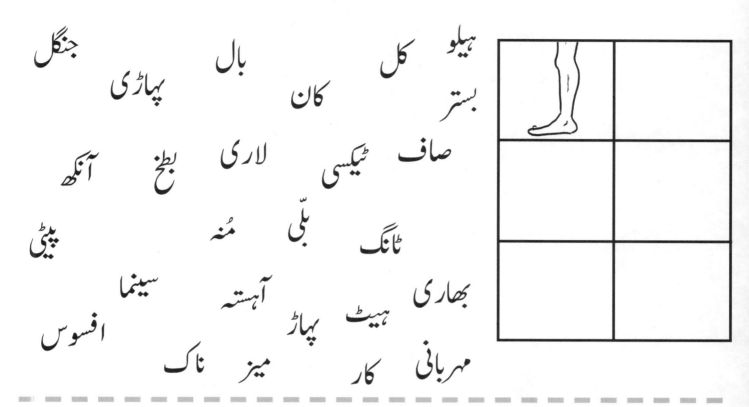

جنگل   کل   ہیلو

پہاڑی   بال   کان   بستر

آنکھ   بطخ   لاری   ٹیکسی   صاف

پیٹی   ٹانگ   مُنہ   بلّی

افسوس   سینما   آہستہ   پہاڑ   ہیٹ   بھاری

ناک   میز   کار   مہربانی

🌀 **N**ow match the Urdu to the pronunciation.

Label the body with the correct number, and write the pronunciation next to the words.

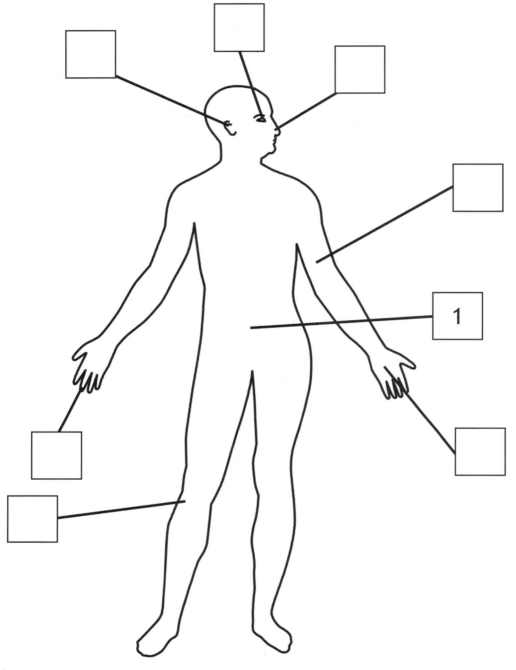

2	بازُو	_____	1 پیٹ _____peT_____
4	ہاتھ	_____	3 ناک _____
6	ٹانگ	_____	5 کان _____
8	اُنگلی	_____	7 آنکھ _____

© **F**inally, match the Urdu words, their pronunciation, and the English meanings, as in the example.

ungalee

hair

Taañg

stomach

پیٹ

hand

بازُو

baazuu

بال

haat^h

پیٹھ

back

اُنگلی

kaan

finger

ہاتھ

arm

ear

کان

peeT^h

baal

peT

ٹانگ

leg

43

❽ USEFUL EXPRESSIONS

Look at the pictures.
Tear out the flashcards for this topic.
Follow steps 1 and 2 of the plan in the introduction.

کہاں ؟ *kahaañ*

ہیلو *hailo*

خُدا حافظ *khudaa haafiz*

نہیں *nahiiñ* ہاں *haañ*

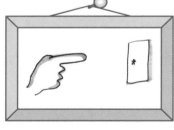

کل (گُزرا) *kal (guzraa)*

آج *aaj*

کل *kal*

یہاں *yahaañ*

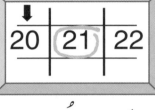

وہاں *wahaañ*

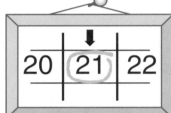

اَب *ab*

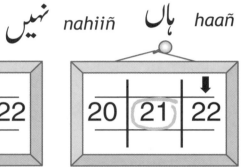

کتنا؟ *kitnaa*

افسوس *afsos*

شُکریہ *shukriyaa*

مہربانی *meharbaanii*

خوُب *khoob*

44

Match the Urdu words to their English equivalents.

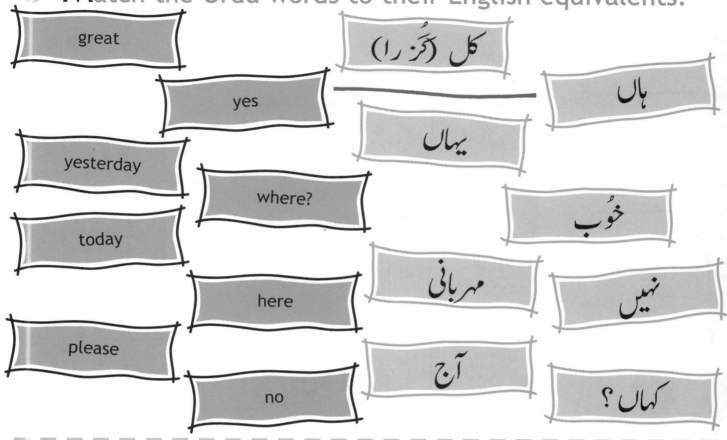

great

yes

yesterday

where?

today

here

please

no

کل (گُزرا)

ہاں

یہاں

خُوب

مہربانی

نہیں

آج

کہاں ؟

Now match the Urdu to the pronunciation.

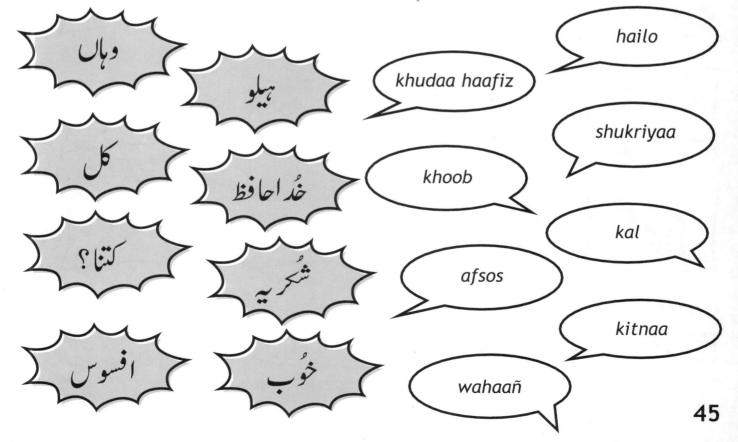

وہاں

ہیلو

hailo

khudaa haafiz

کل

خُدا حافظ

shukriyaa

khoob

کتنا ؟

شُکریہ

kal

afsos

افسوس

خُوب

kitnaa

wahaañ

45

Choose the Urdu word that matches the picture to fill in the English word at the bottom of the page.

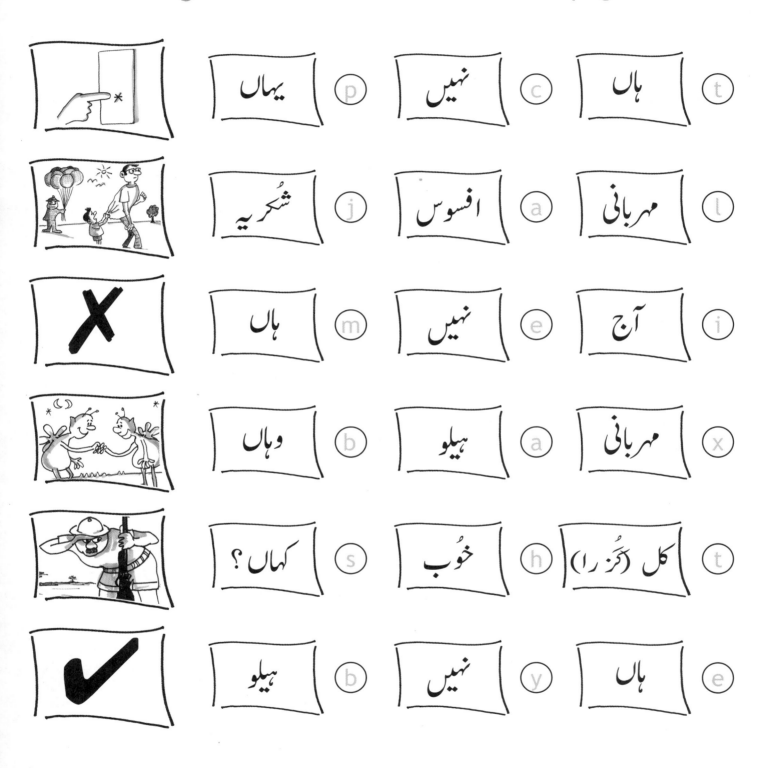

یہاں ⓟ	نہیں ⓒ	ہاں ⓣ
شکریہ ⓙ	افسوس ⓐ	مہربانی ⓛ
ہاں ⓜ	نہیں ⓔ	آج ⓘ
وہاں ⓑ	ہیلو ⓐ	مہربانی ⓧ
کہاں؟ ⓢ	خُوب ⓗ	کل (گُزرا) ⓣ
ہیلو ⓑ	نہیں ⓨ	ہاں ⓔ

English word:

What are these people saying? Write the correct number in each speech bubble, as in the example.

4 نہیں   3 ہاں   2 مہربانی   1 ہیلو

8 کتنا؟   7 کہاں؟   6 افسوس   5 یہاں

Finally, match the Urdu words, their pronunciation, and the English meanings, as in the example.

shukriyaa

hello

afsos

please

وہاں

thank you

یہاں

wahaañ

کل

kal

نہیں

sorry

افسوس

haañ

مہربانی

no

there

yes

ہاں

meharbaanii

hailo

شُکریہ

tomorrow

nahiiñ

● ROUND-UP

This section is designed to review all the 100 words you have met in the different topics. It is a good idea to test yourself with your flashcards before trying this section.

◎ These ten objects are hidden in the picture. Can you find and circle them?

دروازہ	پُھول	بستر	کوٹ	ہیٹ
بائیسکل	کُرسی	کُتّا	مچھلی	جُراب

See if you can remember all these words.

آج
لاری
تیز
ناک
صحرا
ہاں
الماری
شیر
لِباس
سستا
دریا
ٹانگ

Find the odd one out in these groups of words and say why.

کُتّا	گائے	میز	بندر

Because it isn't an animal.

کار	لاری	ریل گاڑی	ٹیلی فون

فارم	کوٹ	سکرٹ	قمیض

سمندر	جھیل	دریا	درخت

مہنگا	گندا	صاف	سینما

خرگوش	بلّی	مچھلی	شیر

بازو	صوفہ	سر	پیٹ

مہربانی	کل (گُزرا)	کل	آج

چُولھا	بستر	الماری	فرتج

◎ **L**ook at the objects below for 30 seconds.

◎ **C**over the picture and try to remember all the objects.
Circle the Urdu words for those you remember.

دروازہ   شُکریہ   جُوتا   پھُول

ریل گاڑی   کوٹ   یہاں   نہیں   کار

گھوڑا   پہاڑ

بستر   کُرسی   ٹی شرٹ   پیٹی

بندر   آنکھ   جُراب   جانگھیا

ٹیلی ویژن   ٹیکسی

Now match the Urdu words, their pronunciation, and the English meanings, as in the example.

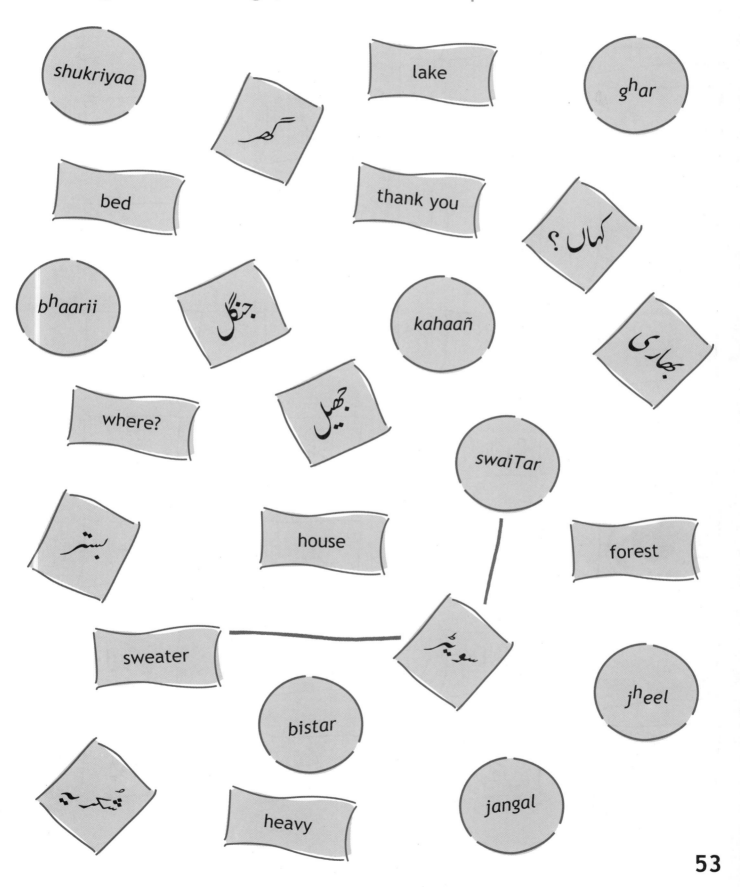

shukriyaa

lake

gʰar

bed

thank you

کہاں؟

bʰaarii

جنگل

kahaañ

جھاری

where?

جھیل

swaiTar

بستر

house

forest

sweater

سویٹر

jʰeel

bistar

جھکی

jangal

heavy

Fill in the English phrase at the bottom of the page.

صوفہ (w)	ٹیکسی (g)	کان (t)
کوٹ (o)	گندا (a)	پُل (e)
ہاں (m)	کتنا؟ (l)	آج (i)
گائے (b)	کھڑکی (l)	ریسٹورینٹ (h)
کہاں؟ (e)	مُنہ (a)	کُتّا (d)
آنکھ (o)	میز (p)	ہیلو (v)
پہاڑی (n)	نہیں (y)	لاری (r)
خرگوش (n)	سڑک (e)	چُولھا (s)

English phrase: w ◯ ◯ ◯ ◯ ◯ ◯ !

Look at the two pictures and tick (✔) the objects that are different in Picture B.

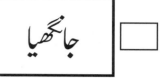 جانگھیا

 ٹی شرٹ

Picture A

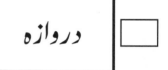 دروازہ

 بِلّی

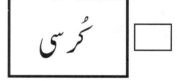 کُرسی

 مچھلی

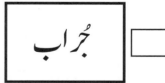 جُراب

Picture B

 کُتّا

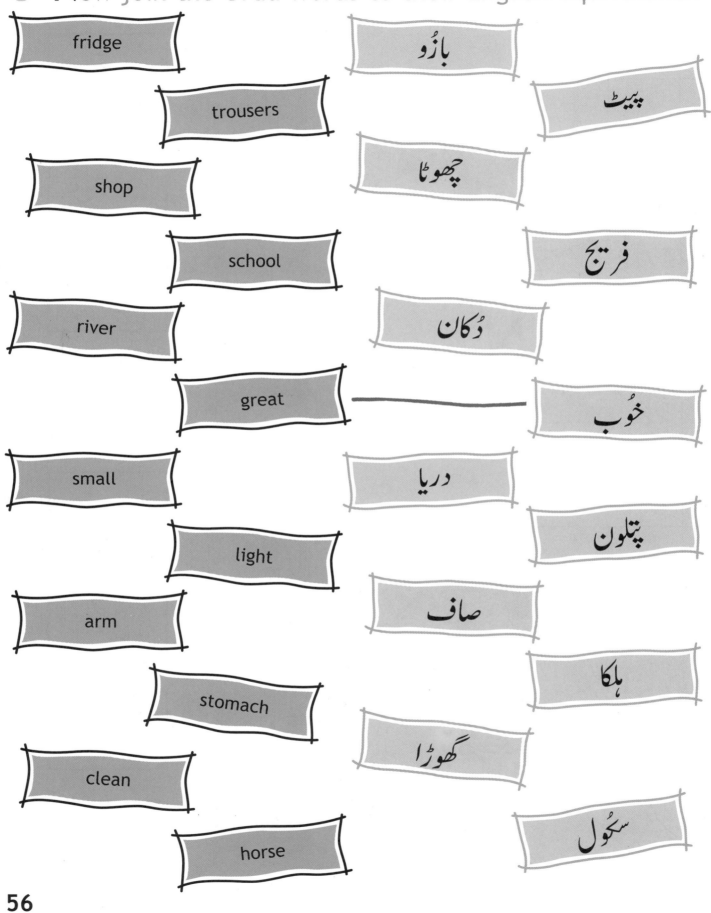

English	Urdu
fridge	بازُو
trousers	پیٹ
shop	چھوٹا
school	فرِج
river	دُکان
great	خُوب
small	دریا
light	پتلون
arm	صاف
stomach	ہلکا
clean	گھوڑا
horse	سکُول

Try to match the Urdu to the pronunciation.

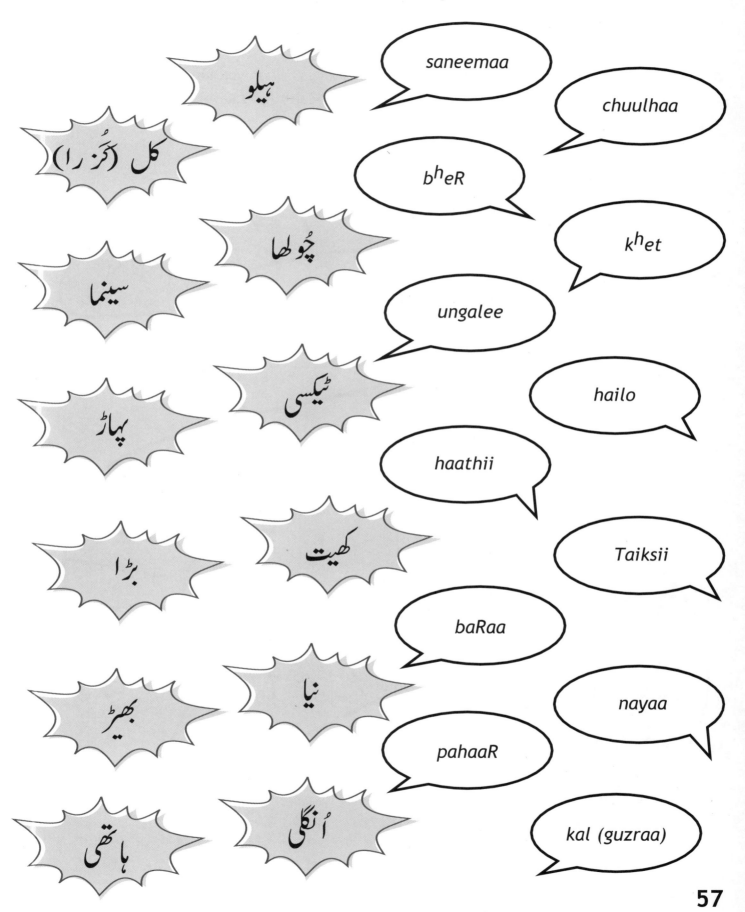

Snake game.

- You will need a die and counter(s). You can challenge yourself to reach the finish or play with someone else. You have to throw the exact number to finish.

- Throw the die and move forward that number of spaces. When you land on a word you must pronounce it and say what it means in English. If you can't, you have to go back to the square you came from.

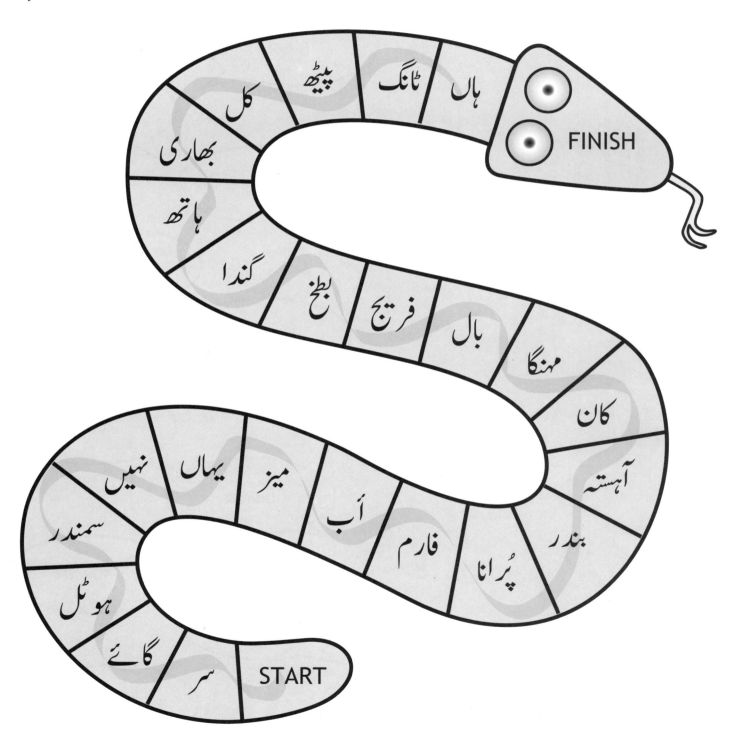

Answers

1 AROUND THE HOME

Page 10 (top)

See page 9 for correct picture.

Page 10 (bottom)

door	دروازہ	table	میز
cupboard	الماری	chair	کُرسی
stove	چُولھا	fridge	فرِج
bed	بستر	computer	کمپیوٹر

Page 11 (top)

میز	mez	کھڑکی	k^hiRkee
الماری	almaaree	ٹیلی فون	Taileefon
کمپیوٹر	kampyooTar	ٹیلی ویژن	Taileevizan
بستر	bistar	کُرسی	kursee

Page 11 (bottom)

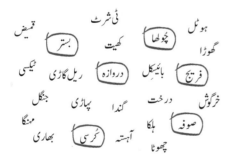

Page 12

Page 13

English word: window

2 CLOTHES

Page 15 (top)

لِباس	libaas	قمیض	kameez
جانگھیا	jaañ^hiyaa	ٹی شرٹ	Tee sharT
جُوتا	jootaa	ہیٹ	haiT
پیٹی	peTee	جُراب	juraab

Page 15 (bottom)

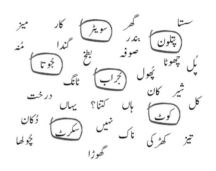

Page 16

hat	ہیٹ	haiT	t-shirt	ٹی شرٹ	Tee sharT
shoe	جُوتا	jootaa	belt	پیٹی	peTee
sock	جُراب	juraab	coat	کوٹ	koT
shorts	جانگھیا	jaañ^hiyaa	trousers	پتلون	patloon

Page 17

ہیٹ	(hat)	2	لِباس	(dress)	1
کوٹ	(coat)	0	جُراب	(sock)	6 (3 pairs)
پیٹی	(belt)	2	سکرٹ	(skirt)	1
جُوتا	(shoe)	2 (1 pair)	ٹی شرٹ	(t-shirt)	3
پتلون	(trousers)	0	قمیض	(shirt)	0
جانگھیا	(shorts)	2	سویٹر	(sweater)	1

Page 18

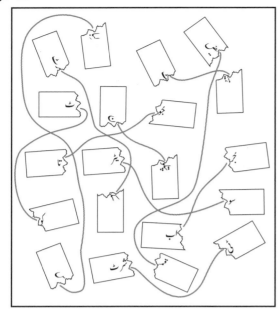

❸ AROUND TOWN

Page 20 (top)

cinema	سینما	car	کار
shop	ڈکان	train	ریل گاڑی
hotel	ہوٹل	school	سکُول
taxi	ٹیکسی	house	گھر

Page 20 (bottom)

bicycle	4
taxi	7
house	2
bus	1
train	6
road	3
car	5

Page 21

Page 22

English word: school

Page 23

لاری	laarii	بائیسِکل	baaisikal
ٹیکسی	Taiksii	ریل گاڑی	rel gaaRi
سکُول	skool	ڈکان	dukaan
کار	kaar	سینِما	saneemaa
ہوٹل	hoTal	ریسٹورینٹ	raisTorainT
گھر	gʰar	سڑک	saRak

❹ COUNTRYSIDE

Page 25

See page 24 for correct picture.

Page 26

پُل	✔	کھیت	✔
درخت	✔	جنگل	✔
صحرا	✗	جھیل	✗
پہاڑی	✗	دریا	✔
پہاڑ	✔	پھُول	✔
سمندر	✗	فارم	✔

Page 27 (top)

پہاڑ	pahaaR
دریا	daryaa
جنگل	jangal
صحرا	sahraa
سمندر	samandar
فارم	faarm
پُل	pul
کھیت	kʰet

Page 27 (bottom)

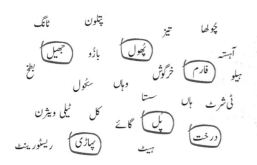

Page 28

sea	سمندر	samandar
lake	جھیل	jʰeel
desert	صحرا	sahraa
farm	فارم	faarm
flower	پُھول	pʰool
mountain	پہاڑ	pahaaR
river	دریا	daryaa
field	کھیت	kʰet

❺ OPPOSITES

Page 30

expensive	مہنگا		dirty	گندا
big	بڑا		small	چھوٹا
light	ہلکا		heavy	بھاری
slow	آہستہ		new	نیا
clean	صاف		fast	تیز
cheap	ستا		old	پُرانا

Page 31

English word: cheers!

Page 32

Odd one outs are those which are not opposites:

نیا   چھوٹا   بھاری

ستا   آہستہ   گندا

Page 33

old	نیا		heavy	ہلکا
big	چھوٹا		clean	گندا
new	پُرانا		light	بھاری
slow	تیز		expensive	ستا
dirty	صاف		cheap	مہنگا
small	بڑا			

❻ ANIMALS

Page 35

Page 36

خرگوش	khargosh		بطخ	batakh
گھوڑا	gʰoRaa		مچھلی	machʰalii
بندر	bandar		شیر	sher
کُتّا	kuttaa		بھیڑ	bʰeR
بلّی	billii		گائے	gaaye
چُوہا	chuuhaa		ہاتھی	haathii

Page 37

elephant	✔	mouse	✘
monkey	✘	cat	✔
sheep	✔	dog	✘
lion	✔	cow	✔
fish	✔	horse	✘
duck	✘	rabbit	✔

Page 38

monkey	بندر	lion	شیر
cow	گائے	elephant	ہاتھی
mouse	چُوہا	cat	بلّی
dog	کُتّا	duck	بطخ
sheep	بھیڑ	rabbit	خرگوش
fish	مچھلی	horse	گھوڑا

❼ PARTS OF THE BODY

Page 40

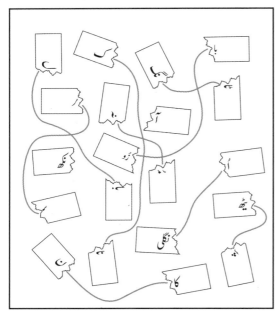

Page 41 (top)

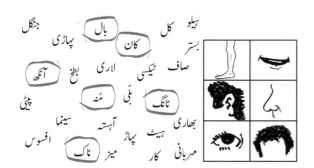

Page 41 (bottom)

سر	sar	بازُو	baazuu
کان	kaan	مُنہ	mooñh
پیٹ	peT	آنکھ	aañkʰ
ناک	naak	پیٹھ	peeTʰ

Page 42

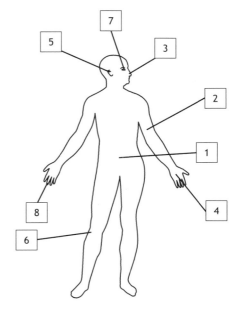

5 کان kaan	1 پیٹ peT
6 ٹانگ Taañg	2 بازُو baazuu
7 آنکھ aañkʰ	3 ناک naak
8 اُنگلی ungalee	4 ہاتھ haatʰ

Page 43

ear	کان	kaan
hair	بال	baal
hand	ہاتھ	haatʰ
stomach	پیٹ	peT
arm	بازُو	baazuu
back	پیٹھ	peeTʰ
finger	اُنگلی	ungalee
leg	ٹانگ	Taañg

8 USEFUL EXPRESSIONS

Page 45 (top)

great	خُوب	today	آج
yes	ہاں	here	یہاں
yesterday	کل (گُزرا)	please	مہربانی
where?	کہاں؟	no	نہیں

Page 45 (bottom)

وہاں	*wahaañ*	کتنا؟	*kitnaa*
ہیلو	*hailo*	شُکریہ	*shukriyaa*
کل	*kal*	افسوس	*afsos*
خُدا حافظ	*khudaa haafiz*	خُوب	*khoob*

Page 46

English word: please

Page 47

Page 48

yes	ہاں	*haañ*	please	مہربانی	*meharbaanii*
hello	ہیلو	*hailo*	there	وہاں	*wahaañ*
no	نہیں	*nahiiñ*	thank you	شُکریہ	*shukriyaa*
sorry	افسوس	*afsos*	tomorrow	کل	*kal*

● ROUND-UP

Page 49

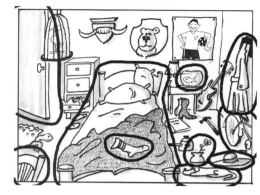

Page 50

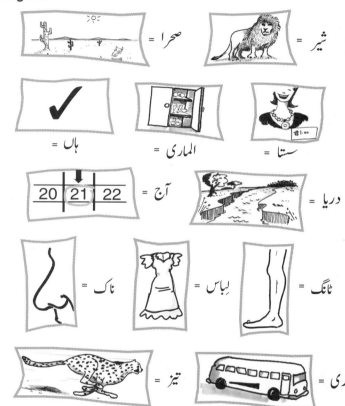

Page 51

میز	(Because it isn't an animal.)
ٹیلی فون	(Because it isn't a means of transportation.)
فارم	(Because it isn't an item of clothing.)
درخت	(Because it isn't connected with water.)
سینما	(Because it isn't a descriptive word.)
مچھلی	(Because it lives in water/doesn't have legs.)
صوفہ	(Because it isn't a part of the body.)
مہربانی	(Because it isn't an expression of time.)
بستر	(Because you wouldn't find it in the kitchen.)

Page 52
Words that appear in the picture:

ٹی شرٹ	بندر
کار	ٹیلی ویژن
پُھول	کُرسی
جُوتا	پیٹی
ریل گاڑی	جانگھیا

Page 53

sweater	سویٹر	swaiTar
lake	جھیل	j^{h}eel
thank you	شُکریہ	shukriyaa
bed	بستر	bistar
house	گھر	g^{h}ar
forest	جنگل	jangal
where?	کہاں؟	kahaañ
heavy	بھاری	b^{h}aarii

Page 54

English phrase: well done!

Page 55

جانگھیا	✔	(shade)
قمیض	✘	
دروازہ	✔	(handle)
بِلّی	✘	
کُرسی	✔	(back)
مچھلی	✔	(direction)
جُراب	✔	(pattern)
کُتّا	✘	

Page 56

fridge	فرِج	small	چھوٹا	
trousers	پتلون	light	ہلکا	
shop	دُکان	arm	بازُو	
school	سکُول	stomach	پیٹ	
river	دریا	clean	صاف	
great	خُوب	horse	گھوڑا	

Page 57

ہیلو	hailo	کھیت	k^{h}et
کل (گُزرا)	kal (guzraa)	بڑا	baRaa
چُولھا	chuulhaa	نیا	nayaa
سینما	saneemaa	بھیڑ	b^{h}eR
ٹیکسی	Taiksii	اُنگلی	ungalee
پہاڑ	pahaaR	ہاتھی	haathii

Page 58

Here are the English equivalents of the word, in order from START to FINISH:

head	sar	ear	kaan
cow	gaaye	expensive	mehangaa
hotel	hoTal	hair	baal
sea	samandar	fridge	freej
no	nahiiñ	duck	batakh
here	yahaañ	dirty	gandaa
table	mez	hand	haat^h
now	ab	heavy	b^{h}aarii
farm	faarm	tomorrow	kal
old	puraanaa	back	peeT^h
monkey	bandar	leg	haañ
slow	aahistaa	yes	haañ

کمپیوٹر

kampyooTar

کھڑکی

kʰiRkee

میز

mez

الماری

almaaree

فریج

freej

کُرسی

kursee

صوفہ

sofaa

چُولھا

chuulhaa

دروازہ

darvaazaa

بستر

bistar

ٹیلی فون

Taileefon

ٹیلی ویژن

Taileevizan

window	computer
cupboard	table
chair	fridge
stove	sofa
bed	door
television	telephone

پیٹی

peTee

کوٹ

koT

سکرٹ

skarT

ہیٹ

haiT

ٹی شرٹ

Tee sharT

جُوتا

jootaa

سویٹر

swaiTar

قمیض

kameez

جانگھیا

jaañgʰiyaa

جُراب

juraab

پتلون

patloon

لِباس

libaas

coat	belt
hat	skirt
shoe	t-shirt
shirt	sweater
sock	shorts
dress	trousers

سکُول

skool

کار

kaar

سڑک

saRak

سینما

saneemaa

ہوٹل

hoTal

دُکان

dukaan

ٹیکسی

Taiksii

بائیسکِل

baaisikal

ریسٹورینٹ

raisTorainT

لاری

laarii

ریل گاڑی

rel gaaRii

گھر

gʰar

car	school
cinema	road
shop	hotel
bicycle	taxi
bus	restaurant
house	train

جھیل

j^heel

جنگل

jangal

پہاڑی

pahaaRii

سمندر

samandar

پہاڑ

pahaaR

درخت

darakht

صحرا

sahraa

پُھول

p^hool

پُل

pul

دریا

daryaa

فارم

faarm

کھیت

k^het

forest	lake
sea	hill
tree	mountain
flower	desert
river	bridge
field	farm

بھاری

b^haarii

ہلکا

halkaa

بڑا

baRaa

چھوٹا

ch^hoTaa

پُرانا

puraanaa

نیا

nayaa

تیز

tez

آہستہ

aahistaa

صاف

saaf

گندا

gandaa

سستا

sastaa

مہنگا

mehangaa

light	heavy
small	big
new	old
slow	fast
dirty	clean
expensive	cheap

بَطخ

batakh

بِلّی

billii

چُوہا

chuuhaa

گائے

gaaye

خرگوش

khargosh

کُتّا

kuttaa

گھوڑا

gʰoRaa

بندر

bandar

شیر

sher

مچھلی

machʰalii

ہاتھی

haatʰii

بھیڑ

bʰeR

cat	duck
cow	mouse
dog	rabbit
monkey	horse
fish	lion
sheep	elephant

اُنگلی

ungalee

بازُو

baazuu

مُنہ

mooñh

سر

sar

ٹانگ

Taañg

کان

kaan

پیٹ

peT

ہاتھ

haath

بال

baal

آنکھ

aañk^h

پیٹھ

peeTh

ناک

naak

finger	arm
mouth	head
leg	ear
stomach	hand
hair	eye
back	nose

شُکریہ

shukriyaa

مہربانی

meharbaanii

نہیں

nahiiñ

ہاں

haañ

خُدا حافظ

khudaa haafiz

ہیلو

hailo

آج

aaj

کل (گُزرا)

kal (guzraa)

کہاں؟

kahaañ

کل

kal

وہاں

wahaañ

یہاں

yahaañ

کتنا؟

kitnaa

افسوس

afsos

اُب

ab

خُوب

khoob

thank you	please
no	yes
goodbye	hello
today	yesterday
where?	tomorrow
there	here
how much?	sorry
now	great